EASTWOOD,
Nottinghamshire

Times past and present

By Harry Riley 2015

*This book is dedicated to a very gracious lady.
World-renowned singer and songwriter Jackie Trent
Patron of Eastwood Booktown Development Group.*

*Whilst visiting us with her husband Colin,
Jackie sprinkled a little of her magical stardust
over our small town, during a too short stay
R.I.P. Jackie Trent
Born 6th. Sept. 1940 – Died March 21st 2015*

Contents

What is there to say about Eastwood?

Well, there is quite a lot say and see and do, with an ever-increasing number of community groups and healthy activities going on, around and about, this wonderfully, gritty old Heritage Town and its surrounding villages.

However this book was not meant to be written, or read, as a student's thesis for a university degree, but more of a celebration of Eastwood, the north Nott's and Derbyshire countryside, and its' many talented sons and daughters, both past and present, in no particular historical order. In effect, it is a labour of love, garnered by the author over four decades of living, bringing up a family, and working amongst the varied and forthright residents. Inevitably there will be omissions, people and places and activities equally deserving of mention, but I hope you will enjoy this brief snapshot of the kind of place and people who inhabit this area, and that you will come back to sample more.

Harry Riley

Chapter 1: The Pub.

Eastwood town has several public houses, each with it's own individual style and flavour. The oldest is claimed to be the Sun Inn. The Old Vaults was built some time later as was The Three Tuns, (once known as the Moon, or the Moon and Stars.) The Wellington Inn, commemorating the great general of Waterloo, commands a splendid central town location. For many years the town also possessed a pub called the Nelson, however this one became a victim of the recession and was closed down, following the fate of the Lord Raglan and the Man in Space. At Hilltop, Eastwood, to this present day, The Greasley Castle is still opening its doors to thirsty customers.

However the Sun Inn is most synonymous with the history of Eastwood.

The large, sprawling, Sun Coaching Inn was built in 1705 and has played an integral role in the development of Eastwood Town.

Throughout the ages, a wide variety of transport has arrived at the doors of this busy Sun Inn hostelry, from wagons and horse drawn coaches, to tram cars and now motorised vehicles.

Indeed, the Sun Inn withstood the many changes that Eastwood itself has endured…as the early Saxon hamlet grew from a few dozen houses into a village, and eventually became the small ex-mining town we know it as today.

Standing at a busy crossroads, this important establishment is uniquely placed to welcome residents, visitors and thirsty wayfarers, to offer comfortable hotel accommodation, drink and refreshments, from national brewery: Greene King.

The Sun Inn has many important links with Eastwood's past, including being referred to in D.H. Lawrence novel Sons and lovers, as the Moon Inn.

On November 19th, 1981 the Mayor of Eastwood, Councillor Mrs. Hazel Braithwaite presented a plaque acknowledging the Sun Inn's importance as the location at which the first steps were taken to create the Midland Counties Railway on August 16th. 1832.

This plaque is on view inside the Sun Inn.

The written text goes as follows:

This plaque was presented to the Sun Inn Eastwood by the Mayor of Eastwood. Councillor Mrs. Hazel Braithwaite on November 19th 1981, to acknowledge the Sun Inn's importance as the location at which the first steps to create the Midland Counties Railway were taken on August 16th 1832 by the coal masters of Eastwood and district.

The Town Council has commemorated that historic decision by including a railway wheel in the Town Council's Coat of Arms, recently enhanced by the addition of a crest to demonstrate more fully the Town's historical significance.

Shown in the framed display is the Town Council's Badge whose design owes much to the work of Councillor Lew Braithwaite. The badge shows the three main aspects of the Armorial Bearings: namely the railway wheel, the black diamonds to signify the Town's early dependence on coal, and the Phoenix to represent the town's position as the birthplace of D. H. Lawrence

Author's note: In 2013, the unprecedented, and possibly never to be repeated, 18 times, Mayor of Eastwood, Honorary Freeman and Alderman of the Borough of Broxtowe, Councillor Mrs. Hazel Braithewaite, sadly passed away, aged ninety.

William the Conqueror's Doomsday Book of 1086, gives Eastwood barely a mention. Eastwood was then known as Eastwick and had a population of less than 200 souls, inhabiting a few scattered houses and farms. (Eastwood Through Bygone Ages by Arthur Coleman) published by Eastwood Historical Society in 1972: ISBN13: 978 0950223407

The book: Eastwood through bygone ages, by Arthur Coleman is believed to be the first one written primarily about Eastwood and provides a fascinating insight into the changes Eastwood endured over the ages, as it grew from a small village into a thriving mining town and how it has relaxed, now the mines have all gone, into a comfortable postal suburb of Nottingham. Arthur Coleman does not rely on known facts and figures, but interviews elderly family members for their personal recollections and is a treasury of social history.

Eastwood and district farms in the early years of the nineteenth century would have been little more than smallholdings, with an acre or too of rotational cereal crop, wheat, barley, sugar beet and potatoes, grown on clayish topsoil, whilst the ground just below the surface was thick with layer upon layer of rich coal, (black gold) required to power the future industrial Revolution.

A typical farm worker could have had two or three jobs, in order to survive and to keep his family together. He might have been described as farmer, quarryman frame-knitter or collier.

There would have been woodland for grazing, lush water meadows in the valley by the winding River Erewash, but by 1850 most of Eastwood Common had become enclosed, as powerful land owners took away the open fields to build rows of brick terraced cottages for miner's families to live in.

Adjacent to Eastwood Town in the Parish of Greasley, the earth becomes red with sandstone, found to be very suitable for brick and pottery making.

In King William's day, Eastwood acres were gifted to William Peverel, believed to be his son, and the man who built Nottingham Castle. The Peveril family also owned lands and property in Derbyshire, notably Peveril Castle at Castleton. (Ref: Arthur Coleman)

Crouched at the top of a windy hill, Eastwood looks out, towards the Derbyshire hills, down and across a green and pleasant valley, where the River Erewash, at times hardly more than a stream, meanders it's slow winding path, eventually to disgorge into the swift and powerful River Trent. From another direction the town looks towards Nottingham City and currently there are efforts to create a tram link from Nottingham direct to Eastwood, in what could eventually become a sleek, modern version of the infamous Ripley Rattler: (notorious tram system that ran from Nottingham, through Eastwood, and on to Ripley in the early part of the 20th. Century.)

Going back in time, we might imagine the Dickensian scene, when, after travelling for many miles through wild, open country and often, narrow, rock-strewn lanes, the horse-driven coaches would pull up, and tired, weary passengers would alight for refreshments…a break and perhaps an overnight stopover at Eastwood.

The horses would be steaming, lathered up and in need of feed, rest and stabling by the permanently live-in team of Sun Inn hostlers, before continuing their journey. Those passengers lucky enough to be sitting snug inside the coach would have had some protection from the weather, but not so, those unfortunates perched up on top, exposed to the extremes of wind, rain and sudden snowfalls. And so in the year of 1705 A.D. the Sun Inn was built at the turnpikes road junction - the busy Eastwood crossroads to Nottingham, Mansfield, Alfreton and Derby.

It was to become an important daily stop for the harum-scarum, Manchester to Nottingham, Mail Coach-passenger-dash, and a market place meeting, for all manner of wealthy and poor folk alike.

Perhaps also it would be a pleasant interlude from a nightmarish journey, through the wild and dangerous countryside, always at risk from violent storms, breakdowns and the plague of desperate highway robbers.

Those rough-crossing winter travels, especially for the unprotected outside passengers, clinging on for dear-life, would have been horrendous.

Often a wheelwright would be called over to the stables, to re-set a broken or damaged axle or to change a wheel. A local farrier/blacksmith would almost certainly have been on permanent standby at the Sun Inn, ready to re-fit a damaged wagon, cart or coach, and speed it's occupants on their way.

Plowman with shire horses, by Eastwood artist Mick Sharp

Chapter 2: The Plough

Many trades would have grown up in and around Eastwood to support the local agriculture and to convert the farmer's crop into saleable products. Thomas Hardy in his famous Wessex novel, The Mayor of Casterbridge, refers to hay-trussers and turnip hoers, and Eastwood would have had it's fair share of these agricultural workers, plus potters, brick-makers, corn millers, maltsters, coopers and hay merchants, basket and hurdle makers, saddlers and cobblers, tanners, and of course there would have been a slaughterhouse-locally known as the knackers-yard. One such building, now a private dwelling, is still to be seen, displaying an old slaughterhouse sign, down by Shipley Lock (only a mile or two outside the town.)

In the old Eastwood Graveyard there is a burial site to a Cordwainer. He would have been a specialist, high-class shoemaker and most probably would have numbered his clients amongst the wealthy landowners from the surrounding counties.

This same burial ground also contains the Lawrence family grave. Although the lettering has been somewhat obliterated by age, Broxtowe Borough Council has thoughtfully provided a marker to guide visitors to the site. The author David Herbert Lawrence is not interred here as he died abroad. Full details of his last resting place, along with many of his works may be obtained from The D.H.L. Heritage Birthplace Museum, situated on Victoria Street in the town centre, or the Library, by the Millennium Clock on Nottingham Road. In addition to that, a visit to Durban House, the D. H. L. Heritage Centre on Mansfield Road (now sadly under closure by Broxtowe Borough Council) is well worth a visit.

Millenium Clock: The Library Centre and the Wellington Inn

D.H. Lawrence Birthplace Museum, Victoria St. Eastwood

Durban House, now D.H.L. Heritage Centre on Mansfield Rd.
(This building was once owned by The Barber Mining Company
and was where D. H. Lawrence's father would collect his wages)

So Eastwood was eventually to grow from a small crossroads hamlet into a larger village, with the addition of the Sun Inn and the market alongside it. Later came other *landmark* drinking establishments such as

The Old Vaults and The Moon and Stars (later to become The Three Tuns Public House.)

Still later with the building of it's nearby canals: The Erewash and the Nottingham Canal, came the boat builders, lockkeepers and canal-side public houses such as the Navigation/Great Northern: Anchor Inn, and the Shipley Boat Inn.

Eastwood's newest pub: The Lady Chatterley, so named after D. H. Lawrence's famous novel.

Turning back the pages of history and stripping away the centuries is never easy, and where there are few visible architectural remains, we have to rely on church records, historical societies, the Internet, and word-of-mouth, family memories. However, we do know there was a tall windmill close by the Sun Inn, and that it's sails would often whirl around at an alarming rate, enough to startle the horses. And where there was a windmill and it's corn miller, there would have been a wheelwright's barn, a blacksmith, and on the outskirts of Eastwood, heading towards Kimberley and Nottingham, a tannery at Giltbrook.

Pentrich hunger marchers passing through Eastwood in June 1817 (by Eastwood artist Mick Sharp.)
Two centuries ago, a windmill such as this, might have stood on Eastwood Common near the Sun Inn crossroads

Above is a nice example of an ancient wheelwright's barn, still in existence in southern England.

Visiting Eastwood market place on any day of the week around the early sixteenth century, and we might have encountered 'hirers-and-firers' men engaged in the process of collecting daily labour for their masters, pie sellers, sadlers, waggoners, cloth weavers, maltsters, quarrymen, stonecutters, lime kiln workers and colliers. There would have been local clergymen and their helpers, and monks from the nearby Beauvale Priory (gifted to the Carthusian Monks by Nicholas de Cantilupe-Lord of Ilkeston, in 1343) and owning much of the local land for two centuries. It would have been a thriving scene as people went about their daily business. Eastwood also had a fair share of Romany Gypsies, tinkers showmen and villiens - freeborn peasants tied or bonded to the lord of the manor. A Gypsy King is buried in St. Helen's churchyard: a Selston Village church. He is listed as Daniel Boswell King of the Gypsies

In the early eighteenth century a typical farm labourer would have been recognised by his loose-fitting smock or tunic of un-dyed hemp cloth, and until the creation of breeches, woollen hose tucked into wooden clogs or hand-stitched boots. His headgear could have been a wide brimmed felt hat or hood. Village women wore long dresses, veils and hats or hoods.

Over time, the farmer eventually gave way to the frame-knitting cottager: Notts, Derbys, and Leicestershire had a great many of these small family businesses.

Using silk, cotton or wool, on small hand frames, men would weave right through the daylight hours whilst their women folk finished off the product by sewing or hand knitting gloves and scarves. Their children had to help by winding wool onto cones. Thousands more agricultural workers were joining the industry as free common land became enclosed. The East Midland counties became the country's hub of lace making: stockings and warm woollen garments. Yet by the 19th century, working men gave up the hose and boot-gaiters, preferring the convenience of trousers. However, the demand for faster, cheaper clothing was insatiable as industry gathered pace. Large weaving frames were invented and these could no longer be accommodated in the small attic or garden room. The cottage industry was doomed.

This naturally had a catastrophic effect on family budgets and created much hardship and poverty. How could a man feed and clothe his family if there was no work. This inevitably led to confrontation and became the birth of Luddism: frame-breaking, and acts of wanton destruction by secret gangs of men, pushed beyond reason into acts of violence.

The workingmen of Nottinghamshire, Derbyshire and Leicestershire were at the front of this lawlessness, that was eventually to lead to The so-called Pentrich Revolution.

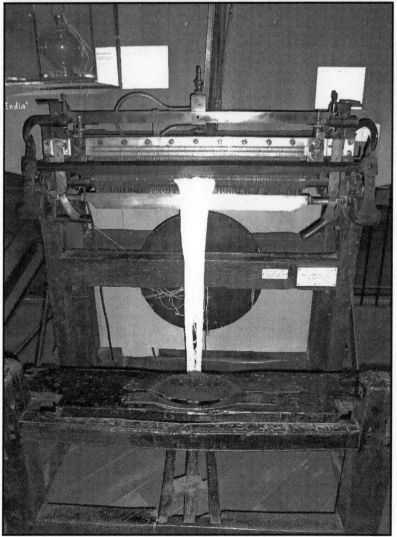

Frame knitting machine at Nottingham castle 2015

Even in good daylight, working a frame-knitting machine could put a tremendous strain on a man's eyesight and he'd be working for a pittance, payment often delayed or paid, not in genuine wages, but in poor quality food by the middlemen-agents.

Chapter 3 The Pit

Moorgreen Colliery. It was closed down in 1985

Factories sprang up and were being constructed in townships. They needed lighting and fuel to power their daily use, and so attention turned to the collier. Bigger and better mines were sunk. Eastwood, north Notts and Derbyshire had coal in abundance, good quality coal seams, that ran on for miles underground and would last for decades. Previously mines had been merely large holes dug in the ground and known as Bell-pits.

And so the cottage hosiery weaver gave way to the collier, and it was to be the late eighteenth and early nineteenth centuries that saw the greatest increase in population that Eastwood had witnessed. It was a time of great change and merciless upheaval with the coming of canals, the railways and the Industrial Revolution.

The early bell or dome pit-shafts were hardly more than deep wells where a miner would be lowered down on a rope-end to where he would begin his daily hacking away at the coal seam. He would start work from early boyhood and be expected to labour long hours, in wet and cramped conditions. Other miners would scratch away at coal just below the surface and fill their buckets in a daily grind. Either way was backbreaking and soul-destroying, with no let-up from work, rest, and with very little play. This would never do for the new industrial era. Fionn Taylor's excellent and regularly updated website, in memory of Philip Healey (Ilkeston Mines Recue1954-1971) http://www.healeyhero.co.uk/rescue/eastwood.htm

Fionn describes Eastwood as a small town in Nottinghamshire where coal has been mined in the area for nearly 700 years and that the monks of Beauvale Priory held rights to coal mining.

He goes into much more detail and lists some of the pits sunk around Eastwood during the nineteenth century as follows:

Barber-Walker Mining Company sank a real vertical mine shaft at Underwood Colliery in 1831. They owned 12 shafts employing 101 children under the age of 13.

Deep mines:

First of the deep mines was **High Park Colliery:** sunk in 1854.

Pye Hill Colliery: sunk in 1874 at Jacksdale and closed in 1985.

New London Colliery: on the outskirts of Newthorpe – closed in 1937

Newthorpe Colliery: on Chewton Street Eastwood, was known locally as Throttleha'penny Pit.

Daykin Colliery: this was on Wellington Place in Eastwood.

Moorgreen Colliery: Owned by Barber-Walker Mining and their most prestigious venture, situated on Engine Lane. It was established in 1865 and closed in 1985, and the site is now commemorated as a nature reserve called Colliers Wood.

Brinsely Colliery: The tandem headstocks were erected in 1872 to service a second shaft. It was here that David Herbert Lawrence's father worked. These distinctive headstocks still remain in a pleasant picnic area, preserved as a lasting tribute to the mine and it's 360+ workforce.

Lodge Colliery: this pit was sunk at Giltbrook and known locally as Billy Hall's Pit. Listed on Fionn's website is a beautiful, hauntingly poignant verse, by a poet, (name unknown to this author) and gives us an insight into a coalminers life at that time:

Billy Hall's Pit

There's a highway running through Billy Hall's Pit

But the coal and the miners have gone.

It now looks a boring landscape

Where once it paid father and son.

It's not that the pit paid good wage

Or conditions were fair to a man.

A coalminers life and being a coalminers wife

Was hard since the pits began.

I've seen them walk the meadow's path

Too tired to spit on the floor.

That long, long journey from Billy's Pit

Up Bridge Street to their front door.

Their faces all black with coal dust

All you could see was their gloom.

Kneepads still fastened to weary legs

With pit boots they walked from the tomb.

That was life in those days at the pit

Working hard for your daily bread.

But now there's a sign in the grass by the road

Saying Billy Hall's Pit is dead.

Plumptre Colliery: so named after The Reverend H.W.Plumptre of Eastwood., was situated between Eastwood Hall and Brinsley Colliery and was closed in 1912.

Watnall Colliery: was sunk in 1873. It was the largest of the coal mines in Watnall and was situated close to the Brickworks. Being closed in 1950.

The Barber Walker Mining Company pay office was Durban House and it was from here that D.H.Lawrence's father would have collected his wages.

(These important mining details were kindly provided by Fionn Taylor. As also was that fine poem: Billy Hall's Pit)

Retired Grocer, Brian Fretwell of Eastwood, remembers Lodge Colliery, known locally as Billy Hall's Pit, this was down Hall's Lane-end, which is now grassed over, High Park Colliery, a deep shaft mine, New London Colliery at Newthorpe, and Daykin Colliery, right in the middle of Eastwoood Town.

He recalls that two local families formed the Barber-Walker Mining Company and sank a deep pit on the outskirts of Eastwood, at Moorgreen, this was followed by many others in the district, such as Brinsley and Babbington and once brought to the surface, this abundant coal had to be shipped to Leicestershire and other Midland counties and then on to London. The pit owners met at the Sun Inn, and in 1832 the Midland Railway was born.

Cocker House-Cocker house Lane

Cocker House is believed to have been built in or around the last quarter of the nineteenth century, on the outskirts of Eastwood, and was doomed to be buried, lost under a mountain of pit waste in the early 1960's, from Moorgreen Colliery underground workings. The Barber family, pit owners, and their top management employees were among its residents. Thomas England and family being the last residents. Mr. England was over six foot tall and according to his daughter Joanne, he spent much of his working life crouched down on the floor, crawling on hands and knees in the dark, the pit roofs underground being so low.

It was discovered that the giant slag/slurry heap, situated near Cocker House was beginning to slide, encroaching ever closer to this beautiful old dwelling and had reached the edge of it's gardens and grounds. Hastily, anything portable, including fittings and fitments were removed and residents evacuated. Then the house was left to its' fate, to be swallowed up and totally consumed by this man-made monster. Later the mound received a top covering of soil and grass in order to help blend it into the countryside. However, rumours still abound amongst the local populace that the mountainous rubble still moves a little each year.

Joanne England, born at Cocker House, was only two years old when this disaster struck, and her family had to leave, but her elder sister Janet, remembers much more:

'The house,' says Janet 'had really large rooms with high ceilings.'

She remembers: 'there being at least seven big bedrooms for residents and guests, separate plus servants- quarters. There were two kitchens, a dining room, lounge-drawing room and snug. Outside the property possessed four stables and large brick greenhouses with heating piped from the house. To the front elevation there were gardens with a croquet lawn.'

Eastwood town grew up around coal mining and I wonder if pit surveyors never foresaw the potential of slurry waste encroaching towards domestic dwellings, particularly on low lying land that had several streams criss-crossing it. It is well known that nearby Coach Drive used to flood with winter rains from a swollen Nether Green/Beauvale Brook.

Also there is a 'mineral' railway line shown on old ordnance survey maps, running from Moorgreen Colliery, passing close by the end of Cockerhouse Road and continuing on to Langley Mill.

By 1965 the Erewash Canal had fallen into a sad state of neglect and was filled in at Langley Mill Basin from Moorgreen Colliery waste, most probably carried along the existing mineral railway line. Five years later along came it's saviours: the Erewash Canal Preservation and Development Association. They promptly set to work with a team of dedicated volunteers and some heavy plant to dig it all out again to restore the basin for narrow-boat mooring and navigation. Their task was enormous but by the grand opening in spring 1973 they had achieved the beautiful result we see and enjoy today.

Again, returning to the question of slurry waste and the seemingly cavalier way it had been tipped and disposed of, we might ask, why did not the Coal Board bosses take account of huge slurry tips being rendered highly unstable and liable to slip and slide during unusually heavy rain conditions, they must have known how heavy rainfall flooded and effected their underground workings, so why so close to housing, as at Cocker House Road. And surely local councils ought to have been aware of these factors too. Eastwood has had its fair share of opencast mining too and now that land is being built upon, along the Eastwood bypass road to Codnor.

If lessons had been learned about colliery waste slippage, perhaps the subsequent disaster at Aberfan, Merthyr Tydfil, Wales, on the 21st October 1966, with such terrible loss of life, might have been averted. The subsequent Public Enquiry laid the blame for that tragedy squarely on the shoulders of the National Coal Board. It was stated the Coal Board had no tipping policy in place at the time. Surely far too high a price being paid for so many lives lost and families ruined.

Chapter 4: The Erewash and Nottingham Canals

The Erewash Canal is almost twelve miles long and was opened in 1779 to transport coal, building materials, agricultural tools, and to carry passengers from Langley Mill junction, along the Erewash Valley to join the River Trent at Long Eaton. It is said the first barge was filled with musicians and colliery masters and as it passed each wharf and bridge a cannon salute and musket fire was made to honour the occasion, in true naval tradition.

The serene Erewash Canal today, lies quiet and peaceful, with little hint of it's boisterous past. Much of the surrounding countryside is little changed, being a haven for wildlife and forming part of the Erewash Valley Trail. The water is clean and clear with an abundance of healthy fish.

From The Langley Mill Basin the canal runs along by the meandering River Erewash, down to Shipley Lock, past the 'Anchor' public house, which is now a private cottage dwelling, and flows on past the Shipley Boat Inn, which has had a name change to become 'MFN,' a favourite bikers meeting place.

Part of the thirty miles long Erewash Valley Trail is valuable wetland and wet meadow corridor for many species of wildlife: birds, insect and aquatic life. A leaflet giving the entire route is available from Broxtowe Borough Council Offices.

 Many different species have been recorded along the entire length of this nature trail: Kingfishers: Finches: Owls; Willow Warblers; Blue Tits and Coal Tits: Tree Pipits: Wagtails: Kestrel; Buntings and Spotted Flycatchers, not forgetting the bats whirling around above as daylight fades into dusk.

The canal aquatic life includes: Carp: Perch: Roach and Pike, Frogs and Water Voles; Mallard Duck: Moor Hen; Coot and Swan, plus Damsel and Dragon Fly.

Along it's banks at various times were Coal Wharves: Water Mills, Corn Merchants: Maltsters: Boat Builders: Farriers and Slaughterhouses (or knacker-yards) as they were known locally.

Several public houses were built along the route to cater for the thirsty canalside workers: the Anchor Inn at Anchor Bridge: The Shipley Boat Inn by Shipley Lock and others along the way towards-Trent-Lock. Can you imagine going back in time to when this tranquil haven would have been quite different. There would have been noisy steam trains crossing overhead and lock keepers chatting away to boatmen and water bailiffs as they went along with their daily chores.

The Nottingham Canal was not fully opened until 1796 with coal and bricks as its main cargo. It was successful and linked in to the Cromford Canal at Langley Mill Basin. A year later the Grantham Canal opened, to cover the 33 miles to Nottingham and joined the River Trent just down stream from The Nottingham Canal. However the canals were now to become victims of their own success, as colliery masters objected to the tolls levied by these local canals, (the brick built Nottingham Canal Toll building is still in existence at Langley Mill Basin.)

Coal Bosses eventually got together to encourage the creation of railways. Thus the canal trade dropped off as the trains were faster and could carry much more freight. It became logical for the canal owners to sell up to the railway rivals and this heralded the end of the Nottingham and Grantham Canals, both falling into disuse and decay. Later local authorities took them over and broke them up by building over large areas. The rest became lagoons and leisure trails for walkers and cyclists, or nature reserves for wildlife conservation.

Now, only the Erewash Canal, which was never owned by the railways, remains navigable for canal pleasure boats from Langley Mill Basin to Trent Lock. This is down to Canal Preservation Volunteers who painstakingly removed the many tons of mining waste from Moorgreen Colliery, which had been dumped into Langley Basin.

Picturesque Langley Mill Basin, as seen in 2015, with the refurbished Nottingham Canal Toll Office to the right side.

Chapter 5: The Pentrich Revolution June 1817

Heaven Knows
Pentrich Martyrs to a cause you fell
You had your say and were locked away
There never was a hope in hell
Harsh masters ruled the day

Heaven knows
With pitchforks, rusty knives and staves
You marched along as sorry braves
And never was a hope in hell
Harsh masters ruled the day

Heaven knows
The years still echo names that cannot rest
Long gone the gallows and the axe-man's blade
Brandreth: Turner: Ludlam, put to test
Harsh masters ruled the day

Heaven knows
To grievous pain and torture you were led
Martyred by a State in fear, lest anarchy held sway
Butchered and bled for a loaf of bread
Harsh masters ruled the day
(Harry Riley)

In June of 1817 thousands of ordinary families were working for a pittance. It was a time of great poverty following the ending of the Napoleonic Wars, with the famous Battle of Waterloo, and the beginning of Britain's Industrial Revolution. Many people could not afford even the price of a loaf of bread and were being cast out of their homes by an uncaring Regency government. Yet the wealthy landowners regularly held lavish fancy-dress parties, where wine flowed like water and it is recorded that the *armed* Pentrich Hunger Marchers stopped at the Eastwood Sun Inn on their way to Nottingham, and asked for refreshments. The Landlady, a Mrs. Godber, recognised one of the leaders, a local preacher: Isaac Ludlam, and castigated him for being involved, beseeching him to return home. He is said to have explained that he would rather be hung drawn and quartered than give up, having come so far. Months later her words, in his case, were proved to be sadly prophetic. He was executed for High Treason, along with two other rebel leaders: William Turner and Jeremiah Brandreth (the so called Nottingham Captain.) Local Author John Dring has written a biography of Jeremiah Brandreth and this is available at a variety of local outlets: including The Pentrich and South Wingfield Revolution Society.

Derby Gaol is now part of a museum privately owned by Richard Felix. The cells would have held Jeremiah Brandreth and the other condemned prisoners: William Turner and Isaac Ludlam.

Prison cell at Derby Gaol: courtesy of Richard Felix.

In a public hanging they were all three, cut down, whilst still alive, and beheaded by an axe-man, outside Derby Gaol, in front of a large crowd. Others were sentenced to hard labour and fourteen local men were convicted and deported to Australia. The marchers had not reached Nottingham, and had only got as far as the outskirts of Eastwood, when they were intercepted by a platoon of the King's Fifteenth Hussars and were dispersed.

It is alleged it had been a government plot to expose and capture local seditionists and to make an example of them.

A government agent; William Oliver, had travelled the north-country, visiting Hampden Clubs in various towns and had encouraged members to believe a general uprising was taking place to overthrow the lawful government and to halt the spread of unemployment and starvation, by forming a new peoples republic. Needless to say, he conveniently disappeared before the court trials. The Poet Lord Byron, from Nottingham's Newstead Abbey, spoke out in Parliament for the starving prisoners, but to no avail. And his friend, visionary poet Percy Bysshe Shelley attended the Derby Public Executions and wrote a considered reflection on the difference between the sudden death a few hours earlier, of Princess Charlotte, and the public outpourings of grief for her privileged rank, as apposed to that of the three condemned rebels: Brandreth, Turner and Ludlam.

2017 will see the bicentenary of the Pentrich Uprising and many local parishes and historical groups along the route taken by those ill-fated and starving marchers, will participate in a variety of cultural talks, walks and re-enactments to commemorate the event. The Pentrich and South Wingfield Revolution Bicentenary Group has galvanised local and international interest and will be producing a weekend of intense activity for June 9th 2017 along with partners: Derby University, Derby County Council, Broxtowe Borough Council, Amber Valley and Erewash Borough Councils. There are plans to re-publish several lapsed editions and to publish several new titles referring to the Pentrich Rebellion, including two by this author: *Twisting In, and other strange tales* and *Butchered and Bled for a Loaf o' Bread.*

Author and local historian Michael Parkin has published books on the subject of the Pentrich Revolution including one about Oliver, the shady government spy, who conveniently vanished during the trials of the captured men.

There will be theatre plays and poetry readings. Awareness talks in local libraries are already taking place. For readers wishing to know more, there are some really in-depth books and articles available on the Internet for downloading to Kindle and other E-readers.

Most of us are aware of the benefits industrialisation brought to this country, but over time that cost was enormous in human suffering and the loss of established trades, trades that had hitherto been considered the life blood of the rural community.

For example, the decline of agriculture came with the Enclosures Act. This was often accompanied by violence and riots, as previous common land was fenced off and enclosed, thus ending the open field system, where a villager could graze his own livestock for free. Peasant farming was effectively brought to an end in England.

The wealthy landowner held the only rights to do just as he pleased. It was the beginnings of capitalism.

The mythical Ned Ludd and Captain Swing were invoked in threatening letters and violent action to smash up and destroy property.

This happened up and down Britain with the Tolpuddle Martyrs and in 1831 Nottingham Castle, (a lavish ducal mansion) was burnt to the ground during rioting against it's owner, the locally-hated and detested Duke of Newcastle, who was apposed to the Parliamentary Reform Act, intended to give all men over the age of 21 the vote. He could see the loss of a large portion of his estates being forfeit and his power draining away.

And so with industrial factories taking over from rural agriculture at Eastwood, as elsewhere, we saw the decline of the millwrights: wheelwrights: maltsters: farriers: tanners: ropemakers: blacksmiths: potters; cottager-frame knitters: candlemakers: charcoal burners etc.

Yeoman farmers had always to wear several hats in order to survive but now they could no longer employ cheap labour. Their peasant workers were forced off the land and into factories, or down coal-mining pits that were being dug ever deeper and wider. Rents had risen and wages had fallen, causing greater inequality. Larger, enclosed farms became the order of the day, to provide higher corn crop yields. Eventually the Yeoman farmer had to give up the unequal struggle and join in the factory queue. In any case a failed crop meant disaster to most rural folk.

The rich just got richer…and the poor, well, they were thrown onto the parish and the workhouse. By this time they had reached the end of the line.

It was considered by government that beggars and the idle poor were holding back the country's progress and causing stagnation (perhaps not unlike the present–day situation.) They should be punished and shown the error of their ways. Author Charles Dickens expressed the situation of the Parish Workhouse very eloquently in his brilliantly evocative novel: Oliver Twist.

The factory masters needed coal to fuel the Industrial Revolution and Eastwood had this in abundance. Very soon there were as many as ten pits around the town. At one time a pit shaft was sunk in what is now the Sun Inn Yard. Two big, important families linked hands and the Barber Walker Company was formed from 1787. They soon owned most of the bigger coalmines in the district.

Previously, in many mines, men women and children under five would be expected to work long hours underground. A Parliament Report in 1842 caused outrage amongst the nation. A child, boy or girl under five could be working twelve hours in filthy water up to their waists, for as little as two pennies a day. They could emerge with terrible deformities.

And now with the closure in 2015 of Thoresby Colliery, (Nottinghamshire's last remaining deep coal mine) local mining historian Anthony Kirby, who worked the Thoresby Mine, has the distinction of becoming the last Eastwood collier.

We have certainly seen trouble and strife within that industry, in the spring of 1984, former Eastwood resident Stephen Page, clearly remembers the 'Battle of Babbington Pit' as the local press described the incident, with flying-pickets gathering at the colliery gates as they attempted to stop miners going in to work. The police struggled to contain this army of truculent miners, as they threw bricks and stones and anything they could lay their hands on. Many arrests were made that day and several police officers were injured. But there was no way the miners could win against a Tory government led by the Iron Lady: Margaret Thatcher. She was determined to smash the power of the NUM and in particular, their President: Arthur Scargill.

And now the coal-fired industrial powerhouse is no more, as Mrs. Thatcher's dream of a country of shop-workers has become much more of a reality, with Nott's and Derby's villages and mining towns laid waste and coal-fired power stations being de-commissioned left right and centre. Eastwood still suffers from cutbacks, due to government austerity measures and voluntary organisations regularly hand out food parcels to hard-pressed families. Have we travelled far in this twenty first century, from those good old days of long ago?

Those good old days would certainly have been good for the fortunate few who had wealthy parents.

45

The poor folk had no National Health Service to assist them when they grew weak through living and working in damp conditions and from subsisting on poor rations.

The Parish Workhouse, when it existed at all, was really there to punish the idle wasters and to shame and discourage them from lazy ways. Woe-betide those unfortunates who became homeless, sick and frail.

Yet through it all, the Eastwood Sun Inn survived and was kept for several generations by the same family of Godbers. There was a time when this public house would play host to magistrate court proceedings, and inquests arising from pit tragedies and sudden deaths, a time when it became a temporary mortuary. There are reputed to be ghosts in the cellars, witnessed by present-day staff.

The history of our tiny island is a story of change and upheaval, some of it gradual, some of it quite bloody, and much of it life-changing.

The small farmer wanted nothing more than to look after his land and feed his livestock, getting his produce to market so that he could feed and clothe his family. It would have been a hard life, working from dawn till dusk, but generations of agricultural workers hoped the sun would never set on their rural way of life.

However change is inherent in the human psyche, and after a bad harvest some would say, what if we could improve the crop, find another way of doing things, make our livestock grow fatter and produce more milk, more meat, store better, keep fresh longer. Meat, fish, grain and fowl. Inevitably mechanisation crept in. The old ways were doomed and the late eighteenth century is believed to be the start of the Industrial Revolution.

Traditionally male work clothing consisted of a loose fitting smock and leggings. These leggings were 'stocking hose' woven from wool and were produced in the East Midlands by framework knitters, using stocking frames and working from home. This cottage industry produced a quality garment, but it was a hard living and the men who worked the stocking frames often became ill, their sight quickly deteriorating from toiling long hours in cramped conditions for very little money. Invariably their families became ragged and poverty stricken. Subsisting on a daily diet of stale bread, rotten potatoes and a weak-mutton-stew.

The whole family would be involved in this laborious work. Women and girls would finish the hose and hand knitted gloves. There was no rest from this miserable, debilitating, backbreaking toil and the lack of sleep and decent food soon began to tell.

Chapter 6: D. H. Lawrence (born 1885-died 1930)

Eastwood is the birthplace of world-renowned author David Herbert Lawrence. He was the son of a miner and caused a great deal of controversy, particularly through his sexually explicit novel: Lady Chatterley's Lover. Today his writings would scarce raise an eyebrow, but in Victorian Britain it caused widespread anger and outrage. Some local people saw themselves in a mirror image of his thinly disguised characters and took offence at what they saw. For years, together with his German born wife: D. H. Lawrence travelled the world, writing his novels, essays, short stories and poetry. He was also an accomplished artist, receiving critical acclaim for his paintings.

Mr. Gary Akers, now in retirement, was a founder member of the D. H. Lawrence society and used to visit America giving talks and slideshows on the writer's life and works. He knew members of the Lawrence family and comments that American literary buffs could never get enough of this exiled author's prolific writings, paintings and poetry.

Gradually the stuffy literary establishment began to wake up to the true value of his talent. Eventually, many years after his death, the name of D.H. Lawrence became mentioned alongside other great literary figures of his time. From out of the coal-dust and the grime had emerged a world-class genius.

He is now rightly recognised as Eastwood's most famous son. The books and learned biographies about him fill many library shelves and modern academics have admitted that during talks about his work they have been accused of scraping him off the ceiling.

In Eastwood we possess a D. H. Lawrence Heritage Birthplace Museum (a shop in the home where he was born.) We also have a blue-line trail along the pavement around the town, linking in to the various homes the Lawrence family once inhabited. There are many bronze plates set into the pavement, bearing quotes from the great man's writing and information display-boards at strategic points. Now in the twenty first century, David Herbert Lawrence has been truly re-habilitated, the establishment claiming him as their own. Durban House, a large red-brick building, once owned by The Barber mining employers, is now the D.H.L. Heritage Centre, containing a mining museum and Lawrence memorabilia (though the fate of this building is continuously in doubt as successive councils struggle with budgets and look for ways to balance their books.)

I often wonder what D. H. Lawrence would have thought about it all? Would he have been pleased to become a great literary symbol, an icon in his native Nottinghamshire? In his own words: *the country of my heart*' or would his rebellious nature have risen up again like the phoenix logo of his books, feeling ill-used and betrayed by the establishment.

The Lawrence family grave is in Eastwood Cemetery
where his mother Lydia and other family members are
buried. His mortal remains do not lie there, as the
inscription incorrectly reads.

Lydia Lawrence, was well educated, and a key force
in encouraging his literary aspirations. She had married
below herself and resented becoming a miner's drudge.

D.H.L. A pavement plaque in Eastwood Town Centre.

(These plaques accompany the blue line tourist trail.)

Chapter 7: Some Churches of Eastwood and District.

St. Mary's Parish Church Eastwood has possessed a church on this site since the seventeenth century. Now only the tower remains, minus the top pinnacles, from an earlier church, mainly destroyed by fire (vandalism-arson by a teenager) in 1962.

Local resident and retired fireman: Don Brown, remembers the fire and recalls how the church was ruined as the roof caved in, only the tower was saved, with the four pinnacles having to be removed, owing to their dangerous condition.

The rest of the building has been rebuilt to a more modern construction and is well used by parishioners for church services and by community, health, and historical organisations. A wide variety of church groups, including a thriving luncheon club, provide comfort, good food and social activities for local residents, and the adjacent Plumptre Parish Hall is in use most of the time.

Incidentally Don Brown was later to receive a gallantry award for his outstanding fire-fighting work. He was commended for rescuing three people from certain death in a horrendous house fire. Not once, but three times he ran back into a dense, smoke filled building to bring out the occupants. In retirement he has published a book called 'Painting and Poetry', and writing of Eastwood, Heanor, Langley Mill and the surrounding area, he gives us a fascinating glimpse of a world we shall never see again.

He remembers the Lawrence family well and has given talks on the subject of David Herbert Lawrence. Don was born in 1925 and has been a long-standing member of

Eastwood Writers Group, currently based at Brinsley Parish Hall.

There are at many churches of other denominations close by, including **Eastwood Baptist church** at nearby Percy Street, celebrating its' 140th anniversary in 2016, declares the incumbent vicar: Reverend. Nick Price.

This church, which, according to previous minister: Revd. John Leigh, traces its origins from Barton in The Beans, has a magnificent full emersion tiled bath for baptising purposes, and has a thriving congregation who also take part in community group activities such as coffee mornings and Knit and Natter clubs. There is also a large conference room where the Eastwood Neighbourhood Watch have regularly held their monthly meetings over several years.

In 1876 when Eastwood Baptist church first opened, at a cost of approx £350.00 Eastwood would have been a very different place to how we know it today. Queen Victoria was monarch of the United Kingdom and Benjamin Disraeli was her Conservative Prime Minister. She ruled alone, as Prince Albert, her young German husband, had been dead for 15 years. For the rest of her life she was in deep mourning for his untimely passing. Victoria's loyal subjects believed the sun would never set on the British Empire, and the following year in 1877 she would become Empress of India.

However it was not until 1902 (after Queen Victoria's death) that children all over the kingdom would wave their little union flags (including this author, growing up in the 1940's) and celebrate the glorious Empire Day. This was on Queen Victoria's birthday May 24th.

In 1876 the motor car had yet to be invented and a loaf of bread could cost around 12 pence. A farm labourer could expect to live to be 45 and earn less than 10 shillings for a fifty five to sixty hour week.

So according to the official 100 years Eastwood Baptist commemorative publication (1876-1976) by F. M. W. Harrison, the Eastwood Baptist Mission started from very humble beginnings, in a cottage on Wellington Street (then known as Step Row.)

Whatever form the 140 year commemoration takes in 2016, one thing is certain, it will have been achieved by many warm-hearted and dedicated people over the years, giving their valuable time and precious resources to build this quiet, community-based Christian Church, right in the heart of their town.

Nobody understands this better than Reverend Nick Price, with his down to earth, friendly and approachable doctrine, bringing together as many local groups as possible through 'The Community Exchange.'

A Roman Catholic church: **'Our Lady of Good Counsel'** is situated at Nottingham Rd. Hilltop, (previously known as Brookhill.)

Lord Kerr, who owned the land at hilltop, was the principal church benefactor. His wife: Lady Cowper, (sister of Earl Cowper) lived at Beauvale House, Moorgreen.

Scottish Lord Walter Kerr was the stuff heroes are made of, and rose swiftly in the navy to become Admiral of the Fleet, being at the relief of Lucknow, during the Indian mutiny.

Monks and parishioners make an annual pilgrimage from this church to Greasley's Beauvale Abbey ruins. A recent community play: 'The Cries of Silent Men' was featured at the Abbey.

St. Mary's Church Eastwood: 2015

Greasley Parish Church of St. Mary has an ancient tower and a beautifully peaceful and well-kept graveyard, containing the remains of some noteable people, including Bejamin Drawater, a surgeon who sailed with Captain Cook on one of his epic voyages of discovery.

Little is left however of the earlier church, as the building has undergone extensive alterations.

*St. Mary's Church Greasley. (Photograph by kind
permission of Anthony Kirby)*

Doreen Lockett, church historian is justly proud of Greasley St.
Mary's and its historical past. During a visit to the church she gave
me a brief snapshot of some of the major features. There is a
stained glass Beauvale Priory Window, bearing the arms of
Nicholas de Cantelupe, provider of Beauvale Priory.

Both families of the Barber Walker Mining Company had close
associations with St. Mary's Greasley. At one time The Barber
family lived at Greasley Castle, adjacent to the church.

St. Mary's has a long history of mining heritage, as displayed in
the Harrison Memorial Window, (dedicated to the memory of John
Harrison-a local colliery manager.) Although the mining
companies agreed not to mine beneath the church this did not stop
cracks appearing in the masonry and the nave breaking away from
the tower.

This meant extensive rebuilding had to be carried out. The cost of this was met by Earl Cowper, the duke of Rutland and the Barber Mining Company. (The story of Greasley Parish Church- compiled by Sarah Seaton MA and Colin Pembleton in 2008.)

The church walls are adorned with monuments to the memory of the church's main benefactors and outside in the old churchyard lie the remains of some very interesting people, as Doreen explains: 'Gilbert Millington of nearby Felley Abbey died in April 1703. Gilbert's father, also called Gilbert, was one of the fifty-nine Regicides who signed the death warrant for the execution of King Charles the First.

When Charles the Second was restored to the throne, many of the fifty-nine commissioners were still alive, brought to trial and sentenced to death. Gilbert Millington escaped abroad. The corpse of Oliver Cromwell was exhumed, along with two of his confederates and hanged at Tyburn, before their heads were hacked off and their skulls impaled at Westminster Hall. This gruesome event is referred to in Samuel Pepys Diary.

Chapter 8: The Langley Mill Basin

The Erewash Canal was opened in 1779 from the canal basin at Langley Mill (linking in to the Cromford Canal) and was intended to ferry coal, stone and building material to the River Trent, at Long Eaton, linking Derbyshire, Notts, and Leics, and running parallel for much of it's length with the River Erewash and the Nottingham Canal, (opened 1796) for the transportation of coal and some passengers directly to Nottingham central. The Erewash Canal was successful right from the beginning and is still navigable, mainly for pleasure longboats, but its commercial viability ended with the coming of the railways in the mid nineteenth century. The Nottingham Canal also suffered as passengers began to opt for the faster travelling by train and is now broken up along the route to Nottingham, into a series of footpaths and small nature reserves along the Erewash Valley.

61

Chapter 9: The Midland Counties Railway

This railway was born at the Sun Inn Eastwood in 1832 by a group of local coal-masters and was to be a means of transporting passengers and coal from Derbyshire to Nottingham and on to Leicestershire, thence to London via the West Midlands, Birmingham lines. The Derby to Nottingham line was opened in 1839. This fast, cleaner transport soon began to see off the canal competition and eventually Nottingham Canal came under the ownership of the expanding railway companies and its decline began. In 1844 two other railways merged to form the Midland Railway.

Eastwood had it's own railway station and there is still a station stop at Langley Mill.

Chapter 10: Beauvale Priory

Beauvale Priory is now a ruin in a farmer's field in the nearby Parish of Greasley. The ruins are in the care of English Heritage because of their historical significance

Today a bright new light shines over a secluded Nottinghamshire valley.

Beauvale Priory Charterhouse Ruins have sprung back into life!

Those sacred, Carthusian stones have been preserved by English Heritage: together with Nottinghamshire County Council for the benefit of us all: religious groups, historians and tourists.

Mr. and Mrs. White, the inspired owners of Beauvale Abbey Farm have now opened the Priory Ruins to the Public with the added introduction of the Gatehouse Coffee Parlour. Guided Tours of the ruins may be arranged by appointment.

Broxtowe Borough Council recently commissioned a community play about the Beauvale Martyrs called 'The Cries of Silent Men.' Another event (extremely well attended) was the tented Medieval Fayre.

The whole weekend show was in glorious costume and monks and minstrels, yeomen farmers and their wives mingled with the crowds, chickens, ducks and geese. Knights and their squires gave combat exhibitions in full *heavy* armour and Pike-men and Bowmen performed field manoeuvres. Visitors could try their hands at archery with the longbow and around the field perimeter were the tents of assorted *medieval* craftsmen displaying their wares.

Reflection's of a visit to a Medieval Fayre

We caught a hint of 'Ivanhoe' at Beauvale Priory's Medieval Fayre and lost ourselves for a while in that heady atmosphere.

'A ruin now, the once proud stone set down, midst Beauvale land
Should haunt the ghost of Henry's vilest past, and taunt him once
again

Those Martyrs set their lives at nought and never yielding, soon were caught

They could have chosen King 'bove God

They could have given 'liegence to a mortal tyrant he-
They could have hailed him as the grace, above their own beliefs

They would have known his minions were too grand
Yet doomed to hang, they would not bow to threats of his demand!'

Centuries slipped away as visitors were welcomed to the cluster of tents: heraldic flags and banners-flying high, proclaiming we had reached the encampment of 'Team Falchion' fourteenth century re-enactment knights: dedicated to the memory of Sir Nicholas de Cantilupe, Lord of Ilkeston and founder of Beauvale Priory, and whose remains lie at rest in Lincoln Cathedral.

The pious knights, squires, levied peasantry and retinue were realistically dressed in the most natural way with artefacts and weaponry genuinely created, to accurately reflect living and working conditions of the time.

We entered a Roman Catholic knight's cosy, circular tent, containing his bed, complete with decorative inner curtain and feather pillows, sheepskin rugs, laid on authentic matting. An iron banded wooden trunk sat just inside the entrance, containing his personal possessions and doubling as a low table. Spread over this, on an embroidered sleeve, lay his strung-bead-Rosary, tankard, and green-bohemian-glass goblets, his sheathed dagger, working knife and wooden food bowl.

We were treated to displays of 'knights, in man to man combat' Squires doing battle, full of enthusiastic violence (if not such skilful moves) archery exhibitions with the longbow and demonstrations of field manoeuvres by fully armed soldiers. These included pikemen and bowmen and the new musketry of the time, loading and firing (we were told these weapons would never catch on - far too slow and ponderous.)

There were yeoman farmers and their wives and monks and minstrels mingling with the crowd.

Robin Hood was alluded to, and *Dougie the Wood,* had his beautifully crafted artefacts on display.

Many other enthusiasts were present, giving displays and selling their medieval wares, including 'The Knights of Skirbeck' from Lincolnshire with interactive displays of food, cookery and games, as well as armour and weapons (all their equipment being freely accessible.)

'Lawrence mentions Beauvale Priory in his novel: 'The White Peacock,' and it is also mentioned in his short story of 'A Fragment of Stained Glass.'

Beauvale Valley has changed little since Lawrence's day and is well worth a visit.

Chapter 11: Brinsley Village

Brinsley Village is situated on the outskirt of Eastwood, along the Mansfield road. It was once a pit village and the headstocks have been left as a permanent memorial to the mine and it's colliers.

A resident of Brinsley: author **Ztan Smith** has published a prolific range of books on the subject of Brinsley and the surrounding parishes. His books contain many of the quirky characters who have inhabited the area, some of them being quite notorious. Ztan's books are sold to support Brinsley Church and are available from the local Post office.

Chapter 12: Cossall Village Church of St. Catherine's.

Cossall is another small, nearby village, that has retained its rural charm and is mentioned by D.H. Lawrence in his novels. His one-time girlfriend (Louise Burrows) lived in the house next the church. In the grounds of this small church is a twelve-foot high marble obelisk memorial to the Battle of Waterloo (erected in 1877) and is inscribed with the names of three local soldiers who fought in the battle. One of whom: Thomas Wheatley; lies buried in the churchyard.

June 19th 2015 saw the Bicentenary Anniversary of the battle and it was commemorated by a special service of remembrance led by Revd. Dr. Andy Lord. The Service was also attended by the High Sheriff Of Nottinghamshire and other V.I.P's.

A commemorative walk to the church, prior to the service, was led by Eastwood Chapter and Verse Group in Partnership with Notts Guided Walks.

 The Cossall Wellington Group was formed consisting of Cossall Parish Councillors: Notts Guided Walks: Eastwood Chapter and Verse Community Group, and Revd. Dr. Lord's church parishioners.

Cossall Village Nottinghamshire June 18th 2015

The time is twelve noon and approximately 150 people: invited guests to a special service at St. Catherine's Church, are gathered to honour three local heroes, participants at the Battle of Waterloo, 200 years ago to the day.

What makes the event even more special was that in 1877, funds were raised to erect a twelve-foot high marble monument inside the churchyard, to these three men, collectively known as the Cossall Giants: John Shaw and Richard Waplington, both of the Life Guards and Thomas Wheatley of the Light Dragoon Guards. J. S. and R. W both perished on the field of battle but T. W. was to return home and to live out his life back at Cossall village, to be buried at a spot under the monument.

The High Sheriff of Nottinghamshire unveiled the monument in 1877 and in keeping with the tradition, Dr. JAS Bilkhu: the present day High Sheriff, came and unveiled a wall plaque at this special Bicentenary Service, presided over by the vicar of St. Catherine's: Revd. Dr. Andrew Lord.

Dr. Jas. Bilkhu: High Sheriff of Nottinghamshire
Note: In 2005 Dr. Jaswinder Bilkhu was presented with
'The Glory of India Award'

Another kind of war

Britons fought, and many died at the Battle of Waterloo

They gave their all-and sometimes more...

Defending King and Country, and the only God, they knew

But later, sheathing weapons, with duty proudly done

Our troops came back to England

Believing troubles over...yet they'd only just begun

And did a grateful country bring her heroes home to fame?

She surely did - those men returned!

With medals struck for injured: dead and dying, fit and lame

Young captains praised their valour, and loudly beat the drum

But the cost of war was mounting: things would never be the same

The nation set to grieving, we had paid a heavy sum

So soon would memory fade, of mighty battles fought and won

When life at home grew full of strife

No aid came from the State, no help for man or wife

No roof to ward off wintry chill, no money, work or fun

No hope for family future, just demoralizing dread

No meat, no corn, no clothes...not even any bread!

Yet no rain befell the rich man, surprisingly enough

With Parliamentary Power, his future was secure

He had his manor, plots of land, and servants by the score

He'd hold his lavish parties, wild and wanton, wicked, wasteful...

Running on and on forever, and as frenzied as before

There'd be no vote for peasantry: no gracious law to grant them more.

So quickly did dissention grow, and spread from town to town
Ned Ludd and all his firebrands would bring the Government down
In northern counties: Nott's and Derby's too, the talk was insurrection
A multitude would now rise up and cause a great commotion
They'd have their 'rights' and seize the Crown
With the hunger march, of the Pentrich Revolution!

The moral, as we all should know, is 'right' is power, and power is might!
And spies can pull the best-laid plans apart
A trial faced the captured men, and transportation too
Heads were wanted for the axe-mans' block, and some would have to roll
The Kingdom needed vengeance, public hanging for the leaders
Brandreth: Ludlam: Turner; was the prosecution call

If history repeats itself, and this tale is the clue
We need not look for answers, for whom to blame: a foot to fit the shoe

It's down to greed and human waste, and spite, and hopeless need
And all the things that made us what we were, and who we are
We envy what we have not got, and tell ourselves that we know
best
It's every man for himself: let the Devil take the hindmost, and
never mind the rest!

Harry Riley 2015

The order of Service was conducted by Revd. Dr. Andrew Lord

Councillor Susan Bagshaw: The Mayor of Broxtowe laid a wreath during the ceremony, as did Councillor Keith Longdon (Mayor of Eastwood) and the lady Chair of Greasley Parish Council.
Anthony Lynch: of the Lifeguards Association also laid a wreath on behalf of the Household Cavalry Regiment.

Dr, Bilkhu unveiled a wall plaque during the outdoor part of the service.

'The Last Post' was brilliantly played by a lone trumpeter, a student from nearby Kimberley Comprehensive School.

After the service, Quentin Raynor, of BBC East Midlands Television, interviewed several members of the congregation and Trevor White of Kingsmill Hospital's Millside Radio did likewise, in order to broadcast to hospital patients at a later date.

The weather was fine and warm and refreshments were served in the grounds outside the village hall, where a further presentation was made to Cossall Parish Council Chairman: Councillor Brian Maloney, by former member of the Household Cavalry: Anthony Lynch and fellow ex-Life-Guardsman: Clive Watson, of a framed citation and two medals, struck by the Household Cavalry Regiment, with apologies for being two hundred years late with the medals awarded to corporal John Shaw.

I asked ex- Life-Guardsman Anthony Lynch how the citation and medals, presented from the Household Cavalry Regiment to Cossall Village, came about, as I felt he had his own story to tell.

' In May 2009, my wife and I made one of our occasional visits to Combermere Barracks in Windsor, home of the Household Cavalry, of which I belonged.

I had spent some time there when called up for National Service (forty odd years previously.)

On our arrival at the Guard Room We were asked to wait for a Mr. John Lloyd. When he came I asked him if his dad was 'Bunker' and John confirmed it was correct.

Bunker was the equivalent of RSM. I replied he had been a *hard* but *just* master, with a regiment to keep under control.

John enquired where I came from and I told him it was midway between Nottingham and Derby.

He said we have a memorial out there.

I was happy to reply that it was at Cossall Village, about three and a half miles as the crow flies from the village where I live. I thought it was amazing, here I am: 150 miles from home and this fellow knows about the monument at Cossall. I suppose it is part of Regimental History as the two village sons were members of the Life Guards, just as John and myself had been. He said the Regiment would be doing something there in 2015 on Waterloo Day.

I kept in touch with John loosely over the next four and a half years and more recently got in touch with an ex-member: Mr. Clive Watson, from Rugely in Staffordshire, who had served with me and who is on the committee of the Life Guards Association.

Clive got things moving, the result being two framed medals and a citation from the Regiment, which was the highlight of the commemoration event on the 18th June 2015 at St. Catherine's Church, following the Service.

It brought the medals back to the village, which the families had never received, owing to the fact the medals were never cast until approx. forty years after the battle.'

Mr. A. J. Lynch

Mr. C. D. Watson

(ex- D Sqdn. The Life Guards.)

Battle of Waterloo Memorial within the grounds of Cossall St. Catherine's Church

A footnote to the story of Corporal John Shaw is that being an ex-boxer and of unusually large physique he became a sculpture's model and it was at one such modelling session that he is said to have met the writer: Sir Walter Scott. Sir Walter took an interest in his army career and after the Battle of Waterloo the great author visited the battlefield and was shown the spot where John Shaw had died and was buried. Later Sir Walter obtained permission for the soldier's body to be exhumed and his skull was kept at the author's Abbottsford home. A plaster cast copy of the giant's skull is believed to be on display in the Household Cavalry Museum at Windsor.

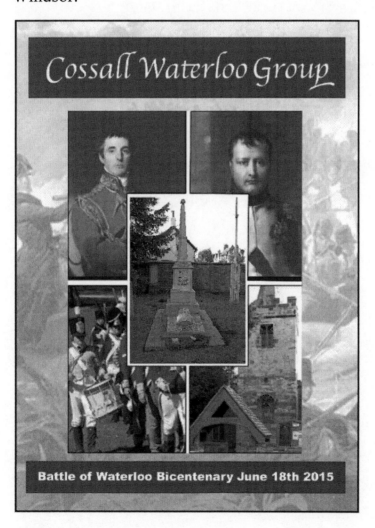

Cossall Waterloo Group

Battle of Waterloo Bicentenary June 18th 2015

Chapter 13: Eastwood's Sporting Heritage

The Astle family of Eastwood raised several boys and one in particular, who became a football legend.

Jeff Astle showed a prodigious sporting talent at an early age and became a player for Notts County at seventeen, under the tutelage of Tommy Lawton. Tommy was the consummate centre forward and he taught the young Jeff all he knew about goal scoring, including how to head a ball for the best effect.

West Bromwich Albion signed Jeff Astle at the young age of 25 and he went on to form an illustrious career with them, becoming known to fans as the King. Jeff was eventually to play for England. The West Bromwich fans never forgot their hero and on Saturday 11th April 2015, some twelve years after his death, the club, now in the Premier League, declared a special Jeff Astle Day, in their league match against Leicester City. The match was a sell-out at west Bromwich Hawthorns ground and Eastwood Mayor: Ken Woodhead was present for the occasion. He was interviewed by Baggies television at the Jeff Astle Gates and the interview was beamed out to the twenty six thousand strong, crowd at the ground. The Eastwood Mayor was mobbed by young fans demanding his autograph, and Ken was also photographed with Laraine Astle: Jeff's widow. In another photograph a young Bangladesh football star joined them. This author was there on the day, and saw first hand the great respect both Jeff Astle and his Eastwood birth town were held.

Brian Fretwell, Eastwood born and bred, and a man who knew Jeff and his family well, was also present and he recalls that fame never changed the footballer, 'Jeff was always the same friendly person he'd always been and who never forgot his roots in the humble mining town of Eastwood.'

Brian also recalls the famous Buckley Brothers, born at Eastwood and both going on to achieve football fame playing and managing.

According to Mr. Fretwell: 'it all began for Jeff Astle in 1942. Jeff was born in a Co-op house on Nottingham Rd. Eastwood, opposite S. Perry-confectioners shop. He was the youngest of five children in the Astle household and attended Devonshire Drive school from age five until eleven.

Headmaster Mr. Spricklehouse, an avid football fan and Notts county talent scout, spotted Jeff's exceptional ability and was able to get the lad on Notts County ground staff at an early age. In those days, Jeff's transport for training at the Magpie's Ground on Meadow Lane, would have been an A4 limited-stop-Eastwood to Nottingham bus. Fellow players would travel back with him. Toney Hately: Dick Edwards and many others would meet up in the local Jack Hardy's Betting shop to discus tactics on how to be on to a winner.

Local lads from the buildings and other Eastwood areas would meet at Mansfield Road Recreational ground for a kick-a-bout. From 2pm onwards, most of them would have been topped up with Shippo's Ale to deaden the pain of a misplaced kick on the shins. Any kind of boot would do: pit boots: farm boots: Wellington boots etc.

Often the boot would fly off and go sailing merrily through the air during the game, which could last for up to three hours and could well finish up with 20-a-side.

Unfortunately for Jeff, he was not allowed to indulge owing to his Notts County commitments. His story was a real-life Roy of the Rovers, boys-own dream come true.'

Pictured are: Mrs. Laraine Astle:
Eastwood Mayor: Ken Woodhead and a young Bangladesh
footballer, outside the Hawthorns West Bromwich Ground on
'Astle Day. June 2015'

Chapter 14: Eastwood Memorials to the fallen of two World Wars

There is a civic parade through Eastwood Town each Remembrance Sunday whereby virtually the whole town's residents turn out in force come rain or shine to honour the

town's fallen soldiers of two world wars. It is a great

uplifting occasion and the young Cadet Groups, Scouts,

Guides and Brownies take part.

They march from the Church after a service to the Town Cenotaph for a formal wreath-laying ceremony and the sounding of 'The Last Post.'

This poem is from John Johnston of Selston, and a member of Eastwood Writers Group.

V.E. Day:

Do you remember V.E. day

So many years ago?

I'll tell you how it was for me,

Perhaps you'd like to know.

The first thing I recalled that day

Was all the church bells ringing

And people dancing in the streets

And cheering: laughing: singing.

 In our little market town

The square was filled with people

And I recall a pair of bloomers

On the high church steeple.

Right in the middle of the square

I saw my Auntie Mabel

It was such fun to see her there

Dancing on the table

While everyone cheered her on,

It really was such fun,

Truly a comic sight

For she was ninety-one.

The people drank, the people cheered,

And strangers kissed each other

My daddy didn't even mind

When someone kissed my mother.

The party carried on all day

The noise was long and loud,

When suddenly a voice was heard

Above the rowdy crowd

A tall man in a dark black suit,

With shining silver hair.

He raised his hands and quietly said:

'Now friends let's have a pause

As we remember those who died

Fighting for the cause.

So for five minutes let us stop

And take a chance to pray

For all our fallen comrades

Who can't be here today.'

And then the square was silent

Not a sound was heard,

No one moved, no one spoke,

Not one single word.

Then as the minutes ticked away

There came a haunting sound:

A piper played a sad lament

Through the silence all around,

And as the last notes slowly died

The square began to clear.

The people started going home

They'd had enough of beer.

So when I think of that great day

It's the piper I recall,

That plaintive, wailing, lingering sound

Really said it all

That those who died won't be forgot

No matter what the years.

God Bless their memory for all time,

Through laughter and through tears.

John Johnston 2015

Chapter 15: The Monkey Run

Another local resident, Helen Sharp of Brinsley Pensioners Group: published author and speaker in local dialects, remembers with affection the courting rites amongst teenage boys and girls in the 1960's. One such ritual, practised most weekends was known as the Monkey Run. Dressed in their most alluring attire, the girls would parade up and down one side of Eastwood town's shop fronts, gazing into the windows as if curious about the contents on display, whilst at the same time coyly sneaking a glance at any boy across the road who happened to catch their fancy. The boys meanwhile would be doing likewise, nonchalantly flicking their hair as they caught sight of the opposite sex in the almost mirrored plate glass. Eventually the lucky ones would pair off. Helen is a writer and often gives Nostalga talks to Care Homes and friendly groups.

Derek J. Taylor is another ex-Eastwoodite. He lived close by D.H. Lawrence family home and won a place at Christ Church college, Oxford. Eventually becoming a journalist he was employed by ITN, reporting on five wars. His book: 'A Horse in the Bathroom' is highly recommended and is about the trails and tribulations of converting an old stables in a picturesque Cotswold Village into a home for him and his wife. It is a great book and full of wonderful humour as he battles with planning laws and even floods while attempting to build his dream home. One chapter of this book is devoted to Eastwood.

Chapter 16: Lord Byron the poet

Lord George Gordon Byron, the Poet was born in 1788.

When barely approaching his teens he inherited the Nottinghamshire Newstead Abbey grounds and estates from his *wicked* great-uncle, and became the 6th Lord Byron. He was educated at Harrow and Cambridge and made his maiden speech in the House of Lords in 1812 supporting the Nott's and Derbyshire framework knitters whose families were literally starving.

Childe Harold's Pilgrimage, his epic poem became a great success and made his name as a serious poet alongside such friends and contemporaries as Percy Bysshe Shelley and William Wordsworth.

Byron later became deeply involved in the Greek fight for independence from Turkish control, spending a lot of his personal fortune in the process to assist the Greek forces.

This British Hero died in 1824 and his body was eventually brought home to rest in the family vault at St. Mary Magdalene Church, Hucknall: Nottinghamshire. His daughter Augusta Ada Byron is also buried there.

Byron also had connections to Annesley Hall through his one-time sweetheart Mary Chaworth. Unfortunately this love affair was blighted and she went on to marry John Musters. Byron wrote a melancholy poem relating to his lost love.

Incidentally a previous Lord Byron had killed one of Mary's ancestors in a violent duel.

In the grounds of the now empty and derelict Annesley Hall stands the ruins of Old Annesley Church. This ruin however has recently undergone a period of intensive tender loving care.

The tower has been made safe and the remaining walls have been neatly topped off. 'The Annesley Old Church Project' has been made possible by local volunteers, with funds provided by the National Heritage Lottery.

Since then, a summer arts and literary festival has been held inside the lawned area of this beautiful old listed building, presided over by local historian: Dr. David Amos, who bore the hands-on task of overseeing the three year long restoration project.

The church ruin stands on a mount and provides glorious views over the Annesley grounds and the valley beyond.

Several of the Chaworth family are buried in the churchyard, including Charles Musters who served on HMS Beagle with Charles Darwin.

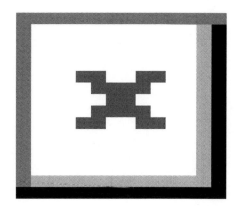

Printed in Poland
by Amazon Fulfillment
Poland Sp. z o.o., Wrocław